Poetry is my praise
A praise that I have for days
A place that I go to
To express how I feel and what others go through

Poetry is my praise
A praise that I have for days
Where I can scream and dream
Release myself in all type of ways

Poetry is my praise
A praise that I have for days
Where I can speak to others
Without being stuck in selfish ways

Poetry is my praise
A praise that I have for days
A place where there is no choice
But to sit and

"Hear My Voice"

Hear My Voice

Speaking Life Through Poetry

☙

Written by Dana English-Nelson

Illustrated & Designed by Naomi Hodawanus

AuthorHouse™
1663 Liberty Drive
Bloomington, IN 47403
www.authorhouse.com
Phone: 1-800-839-8640

First published by AuthorHouse 9/16/09

ISBN: 978-1-4490-2953-1 (e)
ISBN: 978-1-4490-2952-4 (sc)

Library of Congress Control Number: 2009909610

Printed in the United States of America
Bloomington, Indiana

This book is printed on acid-free paper.

All quotes are written by the author, Dana Nelson.

All Scripture quotations are taken from the Holy Bible, New International Version® copyright © 1973, 1978, 1984 International Bible Society. Used by permission of Zondervan. All rights reserved.

Illustrations and Cover Design by Naomi Hodawanus.

Acknowledgments

With my all and everything that is within me, I thank God. I thank Him for all that I am and all that He is allowing me to be. I thank Him for the past, the present, and the future. Thank you Lord for allowing me to see my first book through. I couldn't have made it if I didn't have faith and trust in you.

Thanks to all the Marines, soldiers, and civilians who have dedicated their lives to serving in the United States of America armed forces. Thanks to my Okinawa family and close friends for being there when I needed you most. To my church away from home, Foster Gospel. You have truly been a blessing to me in so many ways. Thanks for allowing me to share my gifts and talents. Thanks to MCCS Entertainment for allowing me to do Spoken Word at the Lyrical Lounge. A special, "Thank you" to Naomi Hodawanus for the illustrations, graphics, and designs. You brought my ideas to life. Another special "Thanks" to Dr. Nettie PerryAdams and Alfred Kennard for taking the time out of your busy schedules to proofread my work.

To my beautiful queens, my mother Rosetta and my grandmother Susie. You are truly awesome women. Your love, strength, and guidance have carried me so far throughout my life and it's because of you that I am who I am today. To my fathers, Truman (Boogaloo) and Francis (Bug). If it wasn't for one of you, there would be no me. If it wasn't for the other you, I would have failed terribly. I'm blessed to have both of you. Thanks to the rest of my family and true friends. Your phone calls and emails have kept me driven.

To my readers, "Thanks for your support." I hope that you continue to follow me as more of my books become published.

To my first love, words cannot express the way I feel when I think of you. Here's a little something that I wrote especially for you.

My First Love

The first time I saw you,
I said, "Wow, he's going to be mine"
You looked into my eyes
I looked into yours
The connection I felt between the two of us,
I've never felt before
I held onto your hand, as you squeezed on mine
Right then I knew everything would be just fine
I want to always take care of you and hold you in my arms
Make sure you're aware of my love and protect you from harm
This love that I feel, I never thought it existed
Love filled with so much joy and happiness
I never thought I would be willing to die for anyone
You're my determination and motivation
You're my first love, my only son

Corez, I want you to know that I am so proud of you. You're everything that I want in a son. Thanks for keeping me on my toes and for showing me how to love willing and unconditionally.

To the man that God gave me to make my life complete, my husband, Andre.
You've rolled with me on this roller coaster ride and I want to thank you
for your patience. Thanks for being supportive and for helping me press
forward. You have love in all the right places.

Love In All The Right Places

You are the vibration of my heartbeat that
makes every rhythm so unique
You are the reason that my knees buckle and get so weak

You are the breath that I take
That keeps me alive and widely awake

You are the push that strengthens me
You help me become what I need to be

You are the water that fills me
When my glass has run empty

You shower me with your love
Baby you keep me happy

You put that smile on my face
That no other can erase

You are the Marine of my fight
You make everything all right

You are the other half that completes me
You are everything that I need you to be

You have all the right ingredients that a real man gives to his woman
You are my lover, my best friend, my loving husband

Dedication

This book is dedicated to everyone that God has placed in my life to help me grow spiritually and to those that have allowed me to turn their lives into poetry.

Table of Contents

Patterns after Patterns
Episodes after Episodes
Knock Downs after Knock Downs
Blows after Blows
When He heard my voice
Slowly I rose

Dilemma

Thoughts of vivid expressions and obsessions
That leads to fatal state of depression
Depression of circumstantial evidence
yet to be known
Pain of life's incidents are embedded
instead of being shown
Substantial increase of blockage within the mind
Release of pressure and facts I seek to find
Attraction of hatred and rebellion
penetrating for years
When there's nothing left but catastrophe
of death to fear
The elevation of anger through trampled
arteries and veins
That plunges the heart with syringes in
excruciating pain

Growing Pains...

"Growing Pains leave stains
Stains that cannot be wiped away from rain"

But Jesus turning to them said,
Daughters of Jerusalem, stop weeping for me, but
weep for yourselves and for your children
Luke 23:28

A Child's Cry

Mama wait don't leave me here
Can't you see it's them that I fear
They do things to me when you're not near
They push me around and have me in tears
I hate it when you go to work
When you leave me they treat me like dirt
I hate these folks and that is no lie
All they do is pick on me and make me cry
I have so much fire burning inside
And you wonder why I never smile
Mama open your eyes
Can't you see
This is not the place I want to be
I kick and scream begging you not to leave
I've held onto your legs
I've even promised and pleaded
I know your job is
important
You've said it many
times
But please love
me first
Look inside this
little heart of mine

Innocent Souls

Children are little innocent souls
They follow while you take control
Pay attention to them
Don't let them slip away
Put them first and save everything else
for another day
Everything you do they are attentive to
They watch what you say and what you do

What you allow determines their outcome
Be aware of their surroundings especially
when their young
Don't be blinded
Know when there's something wrong
Make sure their reactions are of the norm
Always know what's going on
They won't understand the reasons why
All they know is that they're hurting inside
Hear your little ones cry

Let Me Be

When my head is down
My legs are straddled and my back is
up against the wall
My ears are covered to block you out
and I don't want to talk at all
It is best to let me be

When my hands are sweaty and
formed into a fist
I have to sit on them in order
for me to resist
It is best to let me be

When my eyes are shut tight and
I don't want to see you
I'm rationalizing the situation
and hoping that it's not true
It is best to let me be

It is best to let me be.....
IT IS BEST TO LET ME BE

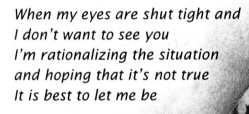

Clutched

I know what he did to you
I'm sorry for what he did

Do you have to constantly remind me of it
I'm just a little kid

The degrading words and the hits
They're really making it difficult for me

I'm your child
I'm not him
I have my own personality

Hopefully
You'll see that one day
When you stop beating him into me

Frustration

Little girl tie your shoe
I'm not going to do it for you
I'm tired of explaining
I'm not telling you twice
The next time you forget
It won't be anything nice
Now pick up your pace
Move right along
I can't wait for your
ride to come
So you can go home

Mistreated

Why do I have to babysit
You act like I'm the one that made it
Why do I have to stay in
You won't even allow me to hang
out with friends
Why do you punish me when
they mess up
They do wrong but you whip my butt
Is it wrong or is it fair
That I'm always feeling like the
dark cloud here
When things aren't done right
I'm always the one you blame
Yet you continue to say that you
love us the same

Little Church Boy

Little church boy why are you here
Is it because it's the other boys that
momma has grown to fear
Little church boy why are you faking
You pretend to be the nicest guy,
but everyone is mistaken

Little church boy why does momma
think I'm safe with you
Is it because your father is the pastor
and you sit on the front pew
Little church boy they don't
even have a clue
You push up on me more than
other boys do

Little church boy they don't even know
You're worst than those other boys
but you don't let it show

Little church boy you're as
scandalous as they come
You sin more than unbelievers
do and then some

Little church boy I never chose you
You may have had others blinded
But I can see clearly through you

If These Walls...

If these walls could talk
What would they say
Would they tell of all the secrets
that you've had hidden away
If these walls could talk
What would you do
Would you try to tear them down to
prevent them from exposing you
If these walls could talk
Would you confess
Would you admit to the truth and
put all those lies to rest
If these walls could talk
How would you feel
Ashamed
Embarrassed
Maybe relieved
Because of all the things that they have seen
Would you stand tall above it all
Or would you recognize that the shadows of
your doubts are your biggest downfall

...*Could Talk*

Restricted

*I hate you because of what you did to me
Instead of loving you
You're my worst enemy
One day my soul would rest and I would finally be free...
Once you're burning in hell where you need to be!
If I've never seen Satan before I've seen him in you
Because a child of God would have never
done the things you do*

Let anger decrease
Let love increase
Learn to control your emotions
Don't let your emotions control you
Have strength within yourself
To love all the way through

Broken Promises

Where are you
Why did you leave
Was I less of what you need
You said you loved me
How true was that
Your actions showed the real facts
A little time here and a little time there
You couldn't spend two hours with me
Yet you were everywhere
You promised me this and you promised me that
You broke most of them
Then expect me to bounce back
Birthdays
Holidays
Graduations
They were all the same
You made up pitiful excuses and tried to explain
You tried to give money in the place of you
How many times do I have to tell you
I don't want your money
I just need you

"Promises are meaningful
Yet should not be made to be broken
It's just emphasis of desperation and small talk
that is softly spoken"

Abandoned

Mama kicked me out
Because of a dude
She said I didn't respect her
And that he thought I was rude
She didn't even punish me first
She just packed my bags
Put five dollars in my pocket
Then sent me out in dirty rags
I didn't say anything
Because she wouldn't have understood
That her boyfriend molested me
Every chance that he could
Instead I just walked away
I didn't dare drop a tear
I was on the road at eleven years old
A kid distressed in fear...

Bloodline

Crooked line

Straight line

Take vital signs

Give injection

There's an infection

We're running out of time

Call his mother

Call his father

We need a matching type

Sorry doctor

His mother is not here

And his father doesn't know what he looks like

Traces

You can't erase the trace
beneath my eyes
And the darkness therein
which leads me to despise
You can't erase the trace
upon my lips
That speaks of you even
though you dipped
You can't erase the trace of
the same blood
Although sometimes you may
wish that you could
You can't erase the trace the
truth is in the mirror
You can deny me if you want but
the picture doesn't get any clearer
You can't erase the trace,
the evidence is there
So stop running
Be a man
Face your fears

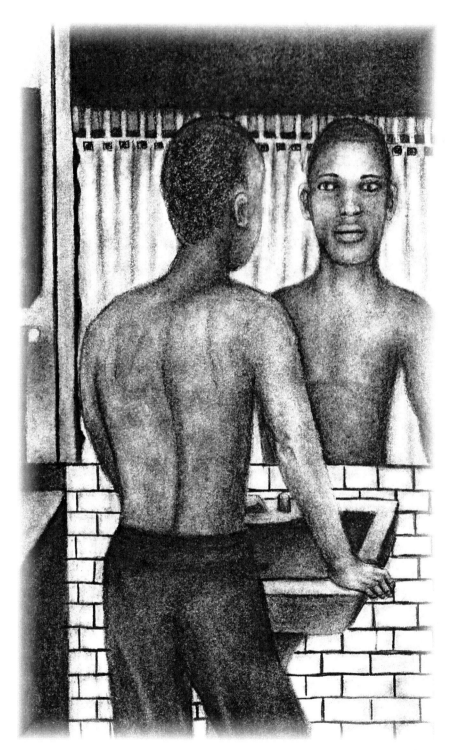

Parents should never abandon their kids
They should own up to what they did

They should do what is right
And bring all truth to the light

Lost Times

So many times we've walked passed each other
Never realizing that we're sister and brother
No one told us anything
Clearly it wasn't our fault
We both were raised up differently
We only knew what we were taught
It never crossed our minds or our thoughts

We're adults now and we've missed so many years
Because of other people's selfish reasons and their fears
It's too late to be upset or shed any tears
All we can do is make up for those lost years

When That Day Comes

I'll dream of you
I'll dream that I'm accepted for
being a part of you
When that day comes
You will see that I'm a younger
image of what you used to be
When that day comes
You'll regret that you didn't know me before
You'll see that I made it without you and
maybe love me even more
When that day comes
It could be bitter or sweet
It will be the very first time that we meet
When that day comes
We may laugh or we may cry
I may even look for answers to understand why
When that day comes
Some things may be at risks
But I'll be happy to know that I'm no
longer just one of your secrets

No matter what the circumstances are
A child is no mistake by far
God already had it in His remarkable plans
Love your child and be a positive role model if you can

The Farmer

You planted your seed a long time ago
You left it for years now you want to watch it grow
That seed you planted you never thought about
You chose to go cropping on a different route
So now that the seed you planted has harvest very well
You want to claim it as if you were always there
Let the truth be told you left it hot and dry
If another farmer hadn't come along it would have died
Now it's too late
So many years have gone by
That seed is now owed by another farmer guy

Never Solo

They may not know you
They may not even care
Don't ever think that you're alone
I'll always be there
Keep your head up and be strong
Remember God is everywhere

Then There Was Love…

"One should never have to question love
when the answer is already there
It's the matter of facing the truth
that you have to beware"

What is Love

Is it you
Is it me
Is it money
Is it something to share
Is it to beware
Is it something that is touched
Is it a feeling that means so much
Is it real
Is it a deal
Is it something to steal
Is it hurt
Is it pain
Is it a name that's used in vain
Is it is something to believe
Do you really know what it means

☙

Love is…
Love is not controlling
Love is not abuse
Love is consoling
So often it gets misused
Love is passionate
Love is kind
Love is fine
It's a genuine feeling that
grows better with time

Falling Petals

As I sit and stare at this beautiful rose
I'm imagining the petals as it grows
The wonderful creation of this flower
Could be gone in less than an hour
I smiled
Thinking of the game I played as a child
He loves me...
He loves me not...
There were so many petals that I've pulled apart
Just to know if he loves me or not
He loves me...
There it goes
Should I let it go or should I catch
it before it falls
Wondering if this man truly loves me at all
He loves me not...
Down went the second one
Maybe I should end it all and just be done
I don't think he knows what it takes to grow
Like the nourishment of the petal of a rose
He loves me...
There goes number three
He says that he loves me
But he doesn't understand me
So how will he ever get to know the real me
He loves me not...
Down went number four
Maybe I should stop
I can't take this anymore
I don't think he understands
what it takes to be a real man
He loves me...
Well....that was number five
The truth still remains it cannot be denied
Could he fulfill all the duties that apply
Will he nourish me like a petal to be kept alive
Or will he pluck away all the remains and let it die

Puppy Love

Often we use the word love for many different reasons
We define it by what the eye finds appealing
Like the money, cars, and diamond rings
Even by the great pleasure that intimacy brings

But...

What happens when none of that remains
Can you honestly say
That you would love that person the same

No Boundaries

Where is it stated
In the book of rules and regulations
That people of different races can't have relations
Where are the documentations of stipulations
That define the laws of their limitations
Is it found in the declarations
Or was it built by different congregations

If you find it, please point it out to me
If it's still not there, then shut your mouth
And let those people be

Black, White, Hispanic, etc...
So what
Love is love
It could be a relationship that was sent from above

Young Love

Love was the best thing during
my younger years
But you took Love away from me
because you were in fear
Fear of me being influenced of
doing something wrong
But Love gave me happiness
Love made me strong
Love was never out to hurt me
It was plain obvious and clear
Love was more than others could be
But you didn't want Love near
Love never tried to change me
Love accepted me for who I was
With Love I could be free
And I never had to be judged
You realized later that Love was true
You knew that Love was real
Love never disrespected you
Love was always sincere

Now you wish you never took Love away
I heard you say it behind closed doors one day
You realized that Love was good for me
But now it's too late to say
Because you turned Love away
Love doesn't live here anymore
Maybe I'll find Love again one day

Blind Love

If you would have said the sky was green
When I know that it's truly blue
I would have believed you

If you would have said planets didn't exist
When it's been proven to be true
I would have believed you

If you would have told me that the sun doesn't shine
That it was only in our foolish minds
I would have believed you

If you would have told me that birds don't fly
That it was just an imagination of mine
I would have believed you

If you would have told me that you'll love me forever
That you and I would always be together
I would have believed you

Deeply In Love

I listen to your heartbeat as you lay asleep at night
I place my head on your chest just to make
sure you're breathing all right

I can feel the rhythm of your heartbeat
as it ponders in my ears
I let the music put me to sleep because
now there is no fear

Oh how I love loving every inch of you
That's why I don't mind doing the things that I do

It's like love for the very first time
I'm so happy that I'm yours and you're mine

The passion and desire runs deeply within my heart
I'll love you until the end of my days
Until death do us apart

❧

Unspoken

I never had the chance to say goodbye
This is why I cry

I never had the chance to say how I really felt
Now I'm beating myself up inside

If only I'd said those loving words
It would have turned everything around
Now it's too late
They will never be heard
Because you're buried in the ground

Dosage of Love

The sun shines outside
Yet it is still dark in here
I can't seem to find my way
I just want to disappear
My eyes are resting heavily
They can't seem to open
My body is here presently
I' m going though the motions
I need a dose of that love portion

Until then...

I am *numb*

I do not *feel*

I do not *hear*

I do not *exist*

❧

Missing Pieces

Without my heart I cannot love you
Without my legs I cannot walk through

Without my bones I cannot stand
Without motivation I cannot win

Without my eyes I cannot see
Without my mind I cannot think clearly

Without my soul I cannot continue to live
Without my hands I cannot give

Without air I cannot breathe
Without cravings I cannot need

Without water I cannot quench my thirst
Without reproduction I cannot give birth

Without food I cannot survive
Without goals I cannot strive

Without love I cannot feel
Without pain I cannot heal

Without choices I cannot decide
Without you I cannot be kept alive

Thirst For You

Like the sound of sweet melodies without
the words
In search of that special song
to be heard

"I thirst for you"

Like flowers in the spring
That have dried out and are
dying for rain

"I thirst for you"

Like a predator in search of its prey
Waiting to fulfill its hunger everyday

"I thirst for you"

Like pain longing to
be healed
In search for medicine
to be cured

"I thirst for you"

Like a crying baby waiting to be fed
Before falling asleep alone in its bed

"I thirst for you"

Like a child who cries out his
precious eyes
As his mother waves and kisses him good-bye

"Oh, how I thirst for you"

Can You Feel Me

Forgive me if I'm not affectionate enough
Maybe I don't know how to feel
Maybe I can't identify love when it's really real
It's not that I don't like you
Because I really care
I never was exposed to it
It's something that wasn't shared
You've always been my best friend
I just didn't receive it as such
You've always been my lover
I just couldn't express it that much
All the kissing and hugging
I'm just not used to it
I know it's hard to believe
I want to be compassionate
So be patient if you will and hopefully
I'll make it through
Just as long as you're with me
I'll learn how to love you

The Response...

You ask me to forgive you for your
lack of affection
My forgiveness has always been there
I just need you to make the connection
You see real love is not something you put on
Like your favorite set of clothes
Because at the end of the day when
you get undressed
You're left naked and exposed
That's why my inner most feelings
I must never hide
I wear it proudly for the world to see
Yeah some may call it pride
You say you were never exposed to it
It just wasn't shared
Stand in front of the mirror
Take a deep look
Can you see it there
You see real love isn't about all the
kissing and the hugging
It's not like the soap operas with the
blue collared husbands
It has nothing to do with the money or how
much he can spend
You see these castrated metaphors have
taunted the image of real men

You are never tasked to do anything that
you are not capable of
Now that I think about it
All I ever wanted was your love
A hug, A tug
Maybe a back rub
Small units of affections to express our love
So your request for patience
I don't really understand
I've always been there for you
I've been that real man
But if its patience you want as
well as hope too
I will support you on that dream of
making it through

CB

...to *"Can You Feel Me"*

Will You

Will you comfort me when I cry
Will you explain to me the reasons why

Will you wipe away my tears
Will you protect me from my fears

Will you catch me when I fall
Will you be there when I call

Will you tell me that it will be okay
Will you turn and walk away

Will you convict me of my sins
Will you look at my heart from within

Will you point out all my flaws
Will you love me in spite of it all

Will you take my hand and walk with me
Will you leave me behind the heels of your feet

Will you be the person that I need you to be
Will you be the one to complete me

Will you be with me for eternity
I'm asking you

Will you...

Will you...

...Will you love me

Fading Love...

"Love don't last always
Some may say
But real love lasts forever
Unless...
You decide to let it fade away"

Dying Love

You promised that you would
never hurt me again
You did
You lied and you sinned
I gave you my love but you
took me for granted
You had my mind so messed up
I felt like I belonged on a
different planet
I gave you my heart
I loved you with my all
You didn't love me enough
Instead you watched me fall
I'm all out of giving
There is nothing else left
Every second I feel like I'm
taking my last breath

Love never leaves a bruise
Love never makes you feel used
Love is without the material things
Love is a feeling that remains

Tough Love

So many hits
So many bruises
Yet so many trips and plenty of cruises
(Loving the luxury)

So much screaming
Cursing and fussing
Yet so much kissing
Hugging and touching
(Making up was always better)

So many days filled with nothing but pain
Yet so many anniversaries with expensive diamond rings
(Diamonds have always been a girl's best friend)

So many years I dealt with all the mental and physical abuse
Yet so many years there was always an excuse
(Maybe if the food was seasoned good enough)

So many days of planning to leave
Yet so many days I stayed and believed
(Wanting things to get better)

So many years of blaming myself that I was the one wrong
Yet so many years of fulfilling his needs
that I forgot about my own
(Putting him first in everything)

So much time that I let slip away
This time it's a brand new day
(I'm awake now)

Enough Has Been Enough

I won't apologize for being tough
You have done more than enough
Of screwing my life up

The divorce papers have been signed
All I want is what is rightfully mine

I've taken back what you stole from me
My heart, my life, and dignity

I'm alive, revised, and ready for the ride
Just give me my things and sign on that dotted line

I'm free now and it feels so great
I'm just sorry that I waited so late

How Can I

How can I look you in the eyes
And tell you that you're the only guy

How can I tell you that you're my heart
When my heart is not totally of you

How can I be true to myself
And still lie to you

Tell me, "How can I"

Love Finale

I came out of the darkness without you
You weren't there when I came through
Like a slave walking free
I was released from you
Bricks have been lifted from off of me
You're gone now and I'm finally free
I hope I never see your face again
You could never be my lover or my friend
So please don't ever enter my space again
Because your second entrance
may be your end

Deuces

I'm no longer going to depend on you
I'm going to go out and do what I need to do
In order for me to pull through
I will and I must give up on you
There's no more hope for us
I've lost all faith and trust
So must time wasted
So much pain
So much knowledge that I need to gain
In order for me to provide for myself
In order for me to restore my health
I need to love myself

Reminisce

I remember when you were understanding
Now you're always angry and demanding

I remember when you were always filled with joy
Now you talk to me like I am a little boy

I remember when we were the best of friends
Now you act as if I'm a distant cousin

I remember when you would get dressed up for me
Now you don't care if I'm around to see

I remember when you were my world
Now it seems like you hate being my girl

I remember when I loved calling you my wife
Now you make me feel like I'm not needed in your life

I remember when....
Can we get that love back again

You Use To ...

You use to open the door for me
You use to look at me seductively
You use to hold my hand as we walked
You use to listen when I talked
You use to take me out on dinner dates
You use to be on time and never late
You use to stay up all night
on the telephone
You use to make me feel like
I was never alone
You use to whisper in my ear and
say sweet words
You use to remain calm and never
shouted in order to be heard
You use to rub my hands and my feet
You use to get excited to see
me when we'd meet
You use to look in my eyes and be satisfied
You use to love being my guy

You use to rub my back after
a long day of work
You use to enjoy my jokes, teases, and flirts
You use to kiss me daily before you'd leave
You use to have faith in me
because you believed
You use to have that desire in your eyes
You use to make me laugh instead of cry
You use to buy me gifts and surprise me
You use to make me feel like being with
you was where I needed to be
You, you, you used to love me

...Love Me

Marked

There's something unique
I want you to see
It's something irreplaceable
that's inside of me

It has a sour taste of
a bitter fruit
It's an apple dried out
without any juice
A tree without water
that has no roots

It's a mark of tissue that has
been brutally torn
It's a permanent mark of
a woman scorned

Scorned

Betrayal is who you are
Disturbed is who I became
Liar you're no truth by far
Feeling is the one to blame
Disoriented is of the mind
Poised by which was mine
Pain is the sword within my heart
Lies are what tore us apart
Hurt is what I feel
Love in you is not real
Danger of radical rage is what I see
Alone is where you need to be
Dysfunctional is stress that lies within me
Deteriorated is how unhealthy my body can be
Broken pieces are what my heart is formed into
Puzzled of confusion is what lies within you
Passion is what it once was
Affection doesn't exist just because
Unfaithful is what describes you
Sad is me because I still love you

Lust...

Love often gets confused with lust
Lust is a feeling that has nothing to do with trust
Trust your instinct and do not rush
The love you think you have could be lust

I'm Feeling You

Your smooth dark skin, gives that
sensational measure
That sends waves through my spine
as I crave for its pleasure

The fullness of your eyes, looks
deeply within my soul
Drives my emotions wild and
so out of control

Those sexy body strides and
those sweet luscious lips
Makes my body yearn for them, as I imagine
tracing them with my fingertips

Your smile, your style, your total profile,
gives me that natural high
I'm overwhelmed with passion when
I see you nearby

Just to think, if you left today or
tomorrow, what would I do
Would I just keep on imagining
Or would I let you know that
I'm really feeling you

Natural High

We can't change the way we feel
It's really hard to explain
We both know the feeling is real
But there's really nothing to gain
Except shame, heartaches, and pain
And driving someone else insane

The vibe is clearly there
We can sense it anywhere
We dare to stare because it isn't fair
It isn't right yet we know what we like
The vibe cannot be denied
The question is, "Are we willing to take the ride"

You know like me being your ride and die chick
And you being my private Slick Rick
We can do whatever
As long as it's a secret
That type of thing
Without the diamond ring

I know you would like that
I bet that you do
Why don't you take me to a place where I can feel you
Like within the depths of those hazel eyes
In which I love to see
Like me being into you and you being into me
So let's just enjoy the ride
Give each other that natural high
That has us hypnotize from our vibes

Relationships...

There are some that are worth keeping
There are some that's there for a reason
There are some that's there through rain, sleet, and snow
There are some that you just have to let go

Where are the ships in relations
The ones that cruise and waves mistaken
To be blown and thrown in any direction
Where are the ones too strong to be affected
And those that sail forward when rejected
Where are....
The ships...
In relations...

True Friends

When you hurt, they cry
When you leave, there are never good-byes

When you make a mistake,
they never turn away
When you argue, they laugh about
it the next day

When you're wrong, they tell you the truth
They don't lie, they're honest with you

They're there to celebrate birthdays,
holidays, and seasons
They're there throughout your struggles,
accomplishments, and well-beings

They have your back and protect you
from strong winds
They are called "True Friends"

Fake Dreadful Friends

All this time I didn't know
All this time you didn't let it show

All this time I spent with you
All this time we were a crew

All this time I thought you were my friend
All this time we were blood and cousins

All this time you wrote him letters
All this time you thought you were better

All this time you knew how much I cared
All this time you wanted him there

All this time you lied to me
All this time I tried not to see

All this time has been wasted
All this time you wanted me replaced

All this time you envied me
Now time has turned into reality
Still it's hard for you to even face me

My Brother, My Friend

I hate to think of you being there
Because it's not where you are supposed to be
I wish you were at home right now
Spending everyday with your family
Things happen and sometimes it's really hard
for us to understand
Know that what you had in mind
May not be in God's plans
Everything happens for a reason rather
we want them to or not
God will put us in a place sometimes
so that we can think smart
You're not a child anymore
You have a family of your own
Turn away from those so-called friends
and leave the negativity alone
You're going to be gone for a little while
but think of it all as a lesson
God is just trying to prepare you to
get ready for his blessings
Don't worry
Keep your head up
Everything is going to be all right
Your family will be taken care of
Together we will get through this fight

Blame The Fame

You're all geared up with fortune and fame
We grew up together
Somehow you forgot my name
We ran the streets and chilled in the
same neighborhood
Now you act like I don't mean you any good
We were like brothers
We took care of each other
Now that you're a star
You don't have the time
I'm far from your sight
And out of your mind

I'm really proud of your success
But I'm disappointed in what you've become
With your attitude I'm not impressed
You seem to forget those that were there
before your stardom

Love of a Limb

I thought it was love
How deeply wrong was I
You left me alone carrying an unborn child

You said that you loved me and forever we would be
But then you made a bad decision that
forced you to leave me

I could say that it was time wasted from being with you
But I know everything happens for a reason
Really they do

I don't regret anything
Even though I sacrificed a lot
My relationship with you was a great lesson taught

I'm no longer that young girl that you once knew
I'm a lot wiser now
Adulthood I grew into

You were young and so was I
I hope life gives you a second chance
For your sake not mine

All That You

Want To Say...

&

All That I

Will...

"One can never trust a liar but being truthful inspires
That is something we all desire
" A Truthful Man And Woman "

Tell the Truth
Lying is no use
Lies will only destroy me and you
Be honest and don't try to lie
Maybe there are things that could be reconciled

Truth Hurts

If you were honest in the beginning
Maybe things could have been worked out
But since you lied about it
There's nothing to even talk about
There's always one lie after another
I can't even trust you
So I'll save both of us the trouble
By saying that we are through

Done Deed

You played on my emotions to get
what you wanted
You took all that I had,
you bragged and flaunted
I thought I was doing a good deed by
taking care of your needs
But you didn't care about me,
you stood there and watched me bleed
Bleed in puddles of emotional
dishonesty and deceit
Because of the lies and promises
that you didn't keep

I thought we were supposed to
be better than that
As long as I can remember,
I've always had your back
But while I'm out there looking out for you
Who was looking out for me
I don't remember you being there
That's not how this is supposed to be

It really hurts to know that you
did me this way
Just know that when you're in need again,
Turn your cheek the other way

Useful Waste

No need to cry over spilt milk
What's done has been done
Just remember the next time to be cautious
Because repetitive mistakes are no fun

No need to cry over spilt milk
Just tighten up your grip
So that the next time you pour it
You won't even leave a drip

Useless Time

Age upgrade in counts
Weight increase by amounts
Time flies by the hour
Pockets seize by the dollar

Clubs and bars are weekend tours
Drinking, drugs, and gambling are endured
Gatherings and cookouts dwell on fun
Arguments or complaints are done by someone

Death, injuries, and conflicts
Happiness of longevity doesn't stick

Furniture is rearranged
Cars may get painted
Folks think life is at a stand still
And they don't even want to change it

Same people
Doing the same 'ole thing
One would think that time doesn't change
Because they're the same people
Doing the same 'ole thing
The same 'ole way
It's a repetitive cycle
Just a different day

"I'm Sick & Tired"

I'm sick and tired of being sick and tired
Trying to be the perfect person that you want me to be
I'm so sick and tired of you always criticizing me
I'm sick and tired of being sick and tired
Of you always telling me what I do wrong
I'm so sick of your judgement
Why don't you just leave me alone
I'm sick and tired of being sick and tired
Every time I turn around
I'm always trying to make you happy
But you still give me a frown
I'm so sick and tired of being sick and tired
Of you treating me the way that you do
I've tried and I've tried
I just can't please you
I'm so sick and tired of being sick and tired
Hoping that I could change you
Who am I kidding
Regardless, you're going to be you
So it doesn't matter what I say or what I do
Now, I'm so sick and tired of being sick and tired
I'm so worn out, I can't even shout
Instead I'll take my kids and my belongings and get out

Priceless

Instead of saying that you're sorry
You go out and do something nice
Just admit to your faults
My happiness doesn't have a price
All those material things
You can take them straight back
Better yet
Trade them in for some love and affection
Think you can handle that

Accepted

You can't change me
I've never tried to change you
Why can't you accept the things that I do

Why do I get the silent treatment
when I go for an outlet
I'm always stuck in the house with
you feeling like an object

I just don't know how much
more of this I can take
We live in the same house and we
don't even communicate

Maybe you need to think about
this and feel what I feel
Because this has gone on for too long
I mean it For Real

I'm tired of feeling neglected and disconnected
When I try to get closer to you
I thought we became one
Remember when we said "I do"
You must understand this is for
better or for worse
Do you remember the vows that we made
Do we need to rehearse

You can either accept me for who I am
or you can just let me be
Because you knew who I was before
you decided to marry me

A Daddy Do Right

You complain if I do right
You complain if I do wrong
What do you want me to do
I'm trying to take care of my own

I pay child support and I don't even complain
I still spend time with my children
Of course, they're carrying my name

They'll have their father
So you don't have to worry
I'm going to help raise them
I'm in no hurry

I love them just as much as you do
So stop trying to keep them away from me
Even though you and I are through
They're still going to need me

Don't use them against me
That's really not okay
You may think you're hurting me
But you're destroying them more
when you behave that way

Now women complain about their kids
not having a good dad
I'm trying to be a real father but you
still make me look bad

Karma

Honestly I would love to confront you
But you're not worth wasting my words to
You keep your distance and I'll keep mine
Then everything will be just fine
You did me wrong but you'll get yours
It's only a matter of time

If The Tables Were Turned

If the tables were turned
Would you accept what you see
Or would you try to remake me
If the tables were turned
Would you give me another chance
After all the lying, cheating, and romance
If the tables were turned
Would you accept my children as your own
Build a relationship with them that's happy and strong
If the tables were turned
Would you respect my religious beliefs
Attend bible study and church services with me
If the tables were turned
Would you have my back whether it's good or bad
Or would you leave me feeling alone and sad
If the tables were turned
Would you take all the mental and physical abuse
Knowing that there is never an excuse
If the tables were turned
Wouldn't you want to feel completed
I'm sure that you do
So tell me why do I feel cheated
When the tables are turned on you

Unequally Yoked

When you need me, I'm there
When I need you, I can't find you anywhere
When you're looking for something, I find
When I need something, you don't have the time
When you want time for yourself, I let you be in peace
When I want to be alone arguments increase
When you're angry, I'll give you your space
When I'm angry, you're all up in my face
When you're stressed, I let you be
When I'm stressed, you put the blame on me
When you're wrong you hate to admit it
You have to always be right
When I'm wrong, I apologize
But we still end up in a fight
I've told you several times I'm not happy
But you won't let me leave
Years have gone by and I no longer believe
You're not the person that I need you to be
I'm tired of pretending when the truth
is staring in front of me
You're a good provider and that is
all I can really say
It's really sad when that's the only
good thing I can replay
All the decisions never include me
They're always made by you
You don't spend time with the kids,
if they don't do what you want them to
I don't think you have any idea what being a
companion and parent is about
So I'm going to leave so you can figure it out

Position Expired

WOW
What role do I play today
You change like the weather
One day we're equal
The next day I'm not on your level
WOW
What role do I play today
One minute you show love at home
Then when others come around,
You want to be left alone
You distant yourself and you cling to them
You don't treat me like family or your friend
WOW
What role do I have to play
Am I your lover tomorrow
Your brother next week
Or just a friend that you kiss on the cheek
WOW
What role do I play today
I'm resigning from my puppet position
I'm no longer your toy on PLAY DAY

Cold Hearted

You're so cold
What happened to
"To have and to hold"

You can't even say, "I love you"
All I hear now is, "What I will and won't do"

You can't even say, "I'm sorry"
When you make a mistake
But I do hear, "We can't even communicate"

You can't even wake up and say,
"Good morning honey"
All I hear is, "Don't go out and
spend too much money"

When you leave, what happened
to the good bye kiss
All I hear is the door closing after
you've been dismissed

Why are you so cold
What happened to you
I wished I'd known you were going to change
Before I fell in love and said I do

Military Spouse

Leave your cover at the door
Transform yourself before
you enter this floor
Whatever issues you had at
work, please leave it there
Don't bring it home honey,
because it's really not fair
If you want to talk, I'm all ears
But don't give me your attitude,
I don't need that my dear
Know the difference of what you do
Leave that military mentality at work
Please don't blend the two
I know work causes you stress
It sometimes makes you restless
Everyday you're fighting for
our country to be the best
And I am so very grateful for
that, I must confess
But don't let it overpower you and
cause you to become heartless
Let me be your stress reliever
and don't be such a louse
It's okay if I run your bath water
and unbutton your blouse
Stop taking everything so seriously
and try lighting up the house
And don't forget to treat me nice,
because I am your spouse
I don't ask for much and I don't
expect anything more
All I ask is for you to leave your
cover at the front door

"To be identified is to acknowledge one's self"

Revealed

Off with the makeup
Peel off the lashes
Remove the earrings
Take off the glasses
Throw away the boots
Face your true roots
Your time is done
No need to fake it
Daylight has come
Now you're stripped naked

In The Spotlight

You're only being exposed
By turning up your nose
Trying to make someone else feel small
When deep inside you're nothing at all
Talking all loud so the attention is drawn
Running your big mouth to make yourself known
Downing other folks like you're the best
When you're no better than the rest
Trying hard to stay on the ladder
As if nobody else should even matter
Always for gossip and for chatter
Then wonder why your friends scatter
So go on ahead and enjoy the sight
Bring your sunscreen
Because things may get heated
while you're in the spotlight

Shining Without The Spotlight

I'm not going to over step you
Because you like to be known
See my head is not in the clouds
I'm not too much to be shown
I'll listen to you boast and brag
Then down me with your thoughts
And talk about what I never had
Because you do and I don't
See all things have been given
And it can be taken away
You need to recognize that
Before it all vanishes one day
Everything I have and done
I count it all blessings
While you're trying to shine
I'm sitting here resting
I'm not trying to be better
I'm doing what I do for me
I don't need the spotlight
I'll give it to you
Because I shine naturally

Judgment

Calls...

Do not judge, or you too will be judged
For in the same way you judge others, you will be judged,
and with the measure you use, it will be measured to you
Matthew 7:1-2

Who are you to Judge Me?

Who are you to judge me and tell me
what you foresee
Saying, I'm just like my daddy, the apple
don't fall to far from the tree
Who are you to judge me and tell me that I'm
just like my mommy
Saying, I'll sleep with any John, Ted,
or Tommy
Who are you to judge me and tell me that I
don't care about nothing
Saying, One day just one day,
I'll care about something
Who are you to judge me and tell me that my
marriage is not that bad
Saying, You better stay with that man
because he's the best you've ever had
Who are you to judge me and tell me that I
should be ashamed
Saying, everything is my fault and I'm the
one to blame

Please tell me who died and left you in charge
The last time I checked there was only one God
You don't know my story,
although you may think that you do
You go ahead, pick out one perfect person
I don't believe that it's you
So why don't you stop judging me and try encouraging me
Then maybe you'll find your own identity
Instead of pointing the finger at others like me

Inside the Mind...

You walk straight by me and you shake your head
You act as if I'm a ghost or the walking dead
You down me with thoughts and say,
"That's a shame"
You forget I am human too, "Hell I got a name"
You don't know where I've been or what I've been through
I can recall many days when I looked better than you
Understand my world and why I do what I do
Take the time to look inside my mind, will you
I don't think like you so don't judge me as such
Obviously my mind is not strong enough
I'm not going to justify my reasons for getting high
I'm not going to make up excuses or tell any lies
The drug decreases my emotional state of mind
It makes me numb and there is no feeling
When I'm high my life has no meaning
I am taken away from life's brutality
And I don't care what people think or say about me
When I'm not high my emotions take over me
I feel when I don't want to
So when you degrade me
I'll just go get high again so I don't have to feel you

I know I should be able to control myself
And yes I'm taking poison to ruin my health
But it's because of people like you who I can't go to
When I finally have the strength to get myself through
You frown, turn up your nose, and
embrace the word "Never"
As if your life is so perfect and you've always been so clever
I didn't know that I was going to turn to that
Life changes people especially when no one has your back
So the next time you call me a drug addict or a dope fiend
Ask yourself one question
"What are you doing to help me get clean"

❧

...of an Addict

Let it Go

I'm so tired of racial grammar and being
judged by the color of my skin
This has grown really old now,
this battle has got to end
All of this nonsense is just a waste of time
and there's really nothing to gain
I'm sure that we'll both get wet
while standing in the rain
If you're dying for blood and I was
your only matching type
Would you lose your life just because
I didn't look right
We were both created by God
He loves us just the same
So let's love each other the way He wants
us to and not be ashamed
This is a new day and time, and we don't stand alone
We've merged into one human race and together
this country will stand strong

Change

When you look at a person
And you don't understand why
they're the way that they are
Don't mistreat them or judge them by far
Sometimes it's complicated and it's
really hard to explain it
Just understand that somehow
they've been tainted

Tainted

Insane, deranged, with hurt and pain
Because daddy never came to share the fame
Of your special days and basketball games
The identity resembles and
you're carrying his name
Yet, you hate the fact that he will never change
Now nothing in your life will ever stay the same
When one relationship ends another one came
Now you're ashamed and daddy's to blame
So you treat everyone like they're all estranged

Connived, deprived, so you tell lies
To hide the marks beneath your eyes
You cry instead of questioning why
This guy has taken and stolen your pride
He makes you feel like dying inside

You feel unworthy of anything good
So you keep your head down instead
of holding it up like it should
You stray away from your family and friends
Waiting patiently everyday for your life to end

Conceded but pleaded to get what you needed
That's the way you were taught
You said it and believed it
So now you're alone and don't
have a man of your own
Because you believe that you can't
do anything wrong

Your life is so perfect and everything is so great
You don't realize that you're not liked
because you're such a fake
Now when the truth is told and
you're staring it in the face
You leave and move away to a faraway place
When the biggest enemy is you
And from yourself you will never escape

Questioned Identity

I could be the one they said
would never amount to nothing
Because momma was a drug addict and
papa was on the street corner hustling

I could be that sister who has a
brother from another mother
Because daddy cheated and
lied with another lover on the side

I could be what some may call an outside child,
for not being in the plan
Because papa slept with momma,
but wore a wedding band on his hand

I could be that battered soul
controlled in bondage and captivity
Because society didn't do anything
when he walked out on my kids and me

I could be that hateful being
angry all the time
Because I let you get close to me and
you took away what was mine

I could be the one who is always sane,
level-headed, and doing just fine
Until those devils play tricks on me and
mess up my mind

I could be that distant tree with branches
sprouting out from all sides of me
Because I'm not settled in my spirit and my mind
is not where it's supposed to be

I could be that young lady who doesn't recognize love
when it's staring me in the face
Because I wasn't surrounded by kisses and hugs,
so my heart has an empty space

I could be that chatterbox that always has
something to say
Because I didn't have anyone there to
listen to me back in my day

I could be the child that's confused about the
identity of my sex
Because I've been exposed by so many things,
it's hard to tell one from the next

I could be the victim of rape that has
never been out on a date
But because he took away my virginity,
men are whom I'll always hate

I could be the female with the most fabulous
job and great career
But you never knew about my failures and the
process it took for me to get here

I could be the spouse that has to play
by her husband's rules
So I'm obedient and submissive yet his
comments are always cruel

I could be the wife that's not pleasing in the
sight of her husband's eyes
Because before the weight there was passion,
now he gives me looks of despise

I could be the one with everything
so rich and unique
Yet, there's always going to be something
to make me feel incomplete

I could be that young lady who tried to
survive while living on the streets
Shoplifted, broke in houses, slept with different men,
just for something to eat

I could be the girl who vowed that would never give up,
because I wanted out of the hood
So I went to college, got a degree, made six figures,
just to prove those folks that I could

I could be that chick who's in love with the
biggest and richest thug
But because he gives me what I want,
it doesn't matter if he sold drugs

I could be that ten year old child,
who mother kicked out for a man
Because she said I caused too many problems
and I just didn't understand

I could be the woman with that sweet and
humble spirit that ministers to everyone
Because I love to share the goodness of
God and how he saved me from the
things that I've done

I could be any of these individuals
and you may not even see
But yet you are so quick to judge
when you don't even know me

A Place Somewhere

There's a place somewhere,
where they don't judge and they don't stare
They just enjoy each other's company and they
always play fair

There's a place somewhere,
where I can express myself
Be free to be me without facing
any crisis and death

There's a place somewhere,
where there is always peace
There isn't any turmoil or hostility

There's a place somewhere,
where pain doesn't exist
There are only joyful moments to
sit and reminisce

There's a place somewhere,
where all wishes comes true
There are fairy god parents there guiding you

There's a place somewhere,
where there's nothing but love
There are always smiles, kisses, and hugs

There's a place somewhere I would love to see
It's a place where they sing and dance gracefully

There's a place somewhere
Could you take me there

A gossip betrays a confidence,
So avoid a man who talks too much
Proverbs 20:19

Peripheral Definition

How would you define her
Beautiful, innocent, or a desperate little girl

How would you define him
Nice, cocky, or maybe a crim

How do you know that you're correct
Have you done your research yet
Or maybe they're just today's subject

Is there a real reason to define a person
When in all honesty, you're not that certain

Certain of elements that they portray
Or even understand why you think that way

Instead you spread rumors and you talk
But you're so quick to get upset,
When someone gives you an insult

The Wrath...

That day will be a day of wrath,

a day of distress and anguish,

a day of trouble and ruin,

a day of darkness and gloom

a day of clouds and blackness

Zephaniah 1:15

Drenched

When it rains it pours
It's like the sound of anger during an uproar
The dark clouds express the aftermath of fire
That transforms to burdens of human's desires
The outraging thunders and lightening as it strikes
Symbolizes the war of good and evil in a battle fight
The sunshine that was once there cannot be seen anymore
Because the dark skies has overshadowed it
And there's nothing to look forward for
When it rains
It surely pours

Lost

There in the mist a figure sits
Longing for something that doesn't exist
Well-rested and balanced on its feet
In search for something to
make life complete
The rock it carries holds plenty of dirt
Like the age of time that starts from birth
The sky is disguised with darkness and rain
Like the inside of the eyes of a
child with pain
Selectively tampered and
straddled by several
While being tortured and judged
because of its level
Blinded by drenched tears streaming
down its face
Evidence is revealed and leaves
an irresistible trace
Wishing for the feeling to be replaced
By an outstretched arm or
a warm embrace
To take away the memories
that's hard to erase
Looking around corners
and behind trees
Searching without facing
life's uncertainties
Moments are gone and now
time has been missed
Because of searching for
something that doesn't exist

Under Games *Pressure*
Practices
Boy scouts

Fix breakfast
Make dinner
Clean up the house

Iron clothes
Groom hair
Mow the lawn

GET UP
Take out the trash
No need to yawn

Meetings
Projects
Deadlines
Studies
Rehearsals
Guidelines

STAY FOCUS
Don't sweat
Smile please

Sad
Upset
There's no need

Emotional
Burdened
Yet no regrets

WAIT
STOP
NOT DONE YET

Relax
Relate
Just breathe

More to come
OH YES INDEED

Legal Lies

I'm angry and I'm mad as hell
From what those crooked cops did
The real story they didn't tell
All the evidence was rigged

I told them the truth
They acted as if they were on my side
It wasn't any use
Because they played me and the other guy

Now I'm serving years
For a crime I did not even commit
They didn't thoroughly investigate the case
They just used false accusations and said that I did it

To think that these cops are really out to "help us"
Yeah right, they're the ones that we cannot trust

To tell them you're innocent is like me destroying you
Because now I'm serving time at 16 years old
for something that I didn't do

Release Me

What is wrong with me
Why am I so sad
Why do I hurt so bad

What is wrong with me
Why can't I be the person that I need to be
Why can't I be loved unconditionally

What is wrong with me
Why I am always so uptight
Why can't I do anything right

What is wrong with me
Why can't I be the mother of a child
Why am I always the one in denial

What is wrong with me
Why am I so angry and mean
Why do I have low self-esteem

What is wrong with me
Why am I so self-conscious about myself
Why do I always fault someone else

What is wrong with me
Why is my patience short with fuse
Why am I always the one accused

What is wrong with me
Why am I always defending myself
Why do I feel like I'm wrestling with the devil himself

What is wrong with me
Why do I always have to be tough
Why do I feel like I'm never good enough

When does this stop....
When does this end....

Crisis

My car payment and mortgage are two months behind
They laid me off and another job is hard to find
Now my credit is getting really bad
My money has gotten real low
I've given up all that I had
I don't know which way to go

To see the looks on my children's faces
When I can't support them on things
Because I don't have the money
Really makes me feel lame

I'm running out of time
My family has to eat
There's no luck with jobs
I'm tired of feeling weak

I want my family to be happy
Doesn't matter what choice I make
So the options are there
I just don't know which one to take
To either be placed on welfare
Or do something the illegal way

Tug of War

Life is like a tug of war
Some fall back
Some go far
Some succeed
Some leave

Life is like a tug of war
Some make it
Some don't
Some strive
Some won't

Like is like a tug of war
It all depends on who's driving that car

I Need You Here

What hurts the most is that you're not here
You're not here to dry my tears
You're not here to speak life into me
You're not here to help me see
You're not here to feel my pain
You're not here to keep me sane
You're not here to mend all the pieces
You're not here to give me increases
I need you so much
You're the only one who really loves me
It's sad not to feel your touch
I'm not in the place I want to be
I'm yearning for love and affection
I'm just not getting it here
I'm in the wrong direction
Please tell me which way to steer

಄

Truce

Where there is passion
There's always pain
When there is pleasure
There's also rain
When there is happiness
There's also joy
Where there are battles
There's lives destroyed
When there is love
There's also hate
When there is life
There's no escape

Imperfection...

Who can say, I have kept my heart pure,
I am clean and without sin?
Proverbs 20:9

Sin

I've done some things
I'm sure you have too
So don't act like you're perfect
And my shoes don't fit you
Sin is sin
It doesn't matter what it is
There's not such a thing as
yours is small and mine is big
We've all fallen short at some point or another
Whether it's disrespecting, envying, or
hating each other
There's no purity or perfection in any of us
The only person who holds that title is Jesus

Repent!
Turn away from all your offenses:
then sin will not be your downfall
Rid yourselves of all the offenses you have committed,
and get a new heart and a new spirit
Ezekiel 18:30-31

The Flesh

Take away my flesh,
it's dirty and weak
Peel it from the top of my head
to the soles of my feet

Tear it from my hands
and don't allow them to touch
Take it away from me
I could lose so much

Peel it from my arms
and don't allow them to embrace
Take it away because it takes
up too much space

Rip it from my eyes
and don't allow them to see
With it I could end up in a
place where I'm not supposed to be

Tear it from my nose
and disable it to smell
It could be disgusting and
cause others to rebel

Peel it from my ears so I cannot hear
Take it away because it
causes me to fear

Strip it from my body
and make me pure as white
I can do without that filth
As long as my spirit is all right

Repentance

Help me dear God, to get rid of these unwanted ways
I don't want to feel like this, I'm praying for better days

Touch my heart, renew my mind, body, and soul
The pain, the hurt, the anger, let it all unfold

Destroy it all Lord and count it all done "In Jesus Name"
Make it known that my life will never be the same

Son, your sins are forgiven
Mark 2:9

Forgive Me Once More

Lied and cheated, done all things to feel completed
Knowing that at home was where I was needed

Walked in this world with bitterness and strife
Didn't care about my life

Separated myself from my very own family
Thought I had nothing, but they had plenty

Always held grudges and hatred in my heart
Wanted to tear my enemies apart

Despised my father because the man was never there
Blocked out the very few memories that we've shared

Loved my mother but we hardly got along
Couldn't stand for her to tell what I've done wrong

Fought my siblings because I was jealous
Instead of getting along, I remained rebellious

Wasn't nice to my neighbors
Never offered or accepted favors

Hurt many people from contacts and dealings
Didn't care about anyone's feelings
I'm kneeling and pleading

"Father forgive me"

Those who live according to the sinful nature have their
minds set on what nature desires,
but those who live in accordance with the Spirit have their
minds set on what the Spirit desires
Romans 8:5

To Be Like You

I want your eyes so I can see
The things that seem unclear to me
I want your ears so I can hear
The words that sound so unclear
I want your mouth so I can pray
About all the things you want me to say
I want your voice so I can be heard
To teach and preach your holy word
I want your hands so I can touch
The things in life that hurt us so much

I want your powers so I can heal
To speak life not death
Cure all sickness
Give good health
In just one simple feel

I want your heart so I can love my enemies
Despite of what they have done to me
To forgive seventy times seven
No matter what the situation may be
To love willingly and unconditionally
Without having any strife in me

I need all these things and I pray that it can be
So that I'll know without a doubt
There's a spot in heaven waiting for me

"Staying Connected"

When anger identifies me
I can't think clearly
And red dots are all that I can see
"Am I Connected"

When being upset makes me stressed
And I'm not in a good mood because I'm depressed
"Am I Connected"

When those fake people and backbiters smile in my face
And I want to make it known instead of staying in my place
"Am I Connected"

When relationships are destroyed and the enemy is pleased
Because I gave him what he wanted and engaged
in his sinful deeds
"Am I Connected"

When I chose to do wrong instead of doing right
Without having a conscious to even think twice
"Am I Connected"

When I'm afraid to make a stand because of critical
judgment from man
And I don't know that God already has my
best interest in his plans
"Am I Connected"

Must I remove all these things that's listed from above,
Connect with God and fall deeply in love
Like an outlet and a cord that's connected when plugged

Should I stay and pray to be connected everyday
Or be disconnected and let the enemy have his way

The decision is easy and well directed
I think I'll be like the cord
By staying connected

Redemption...

But you, O Sovereign Lord, deal well with me
for your name's sake, out of the goodness of your love, deliver me
Psalm 109:21

It Doesn't Matter

It doesn't matter how much love you give me
or how many gifts I receive
It doesn't matter what you try to do to
make sure that I'm pleased
"It doesn't matter"

It doesn't matter how many times you lend
your shoulder for me to cry on
Or how many times you told me to keep
my head up and be strong
"It doesn't matter"

It doesn't matter how many degrees I have
displayed on the wall
Or if I'm well known at the city hall
"It doesn't matter"

It doesn't matter how many fancy cars that I drive
Or how beautiful my house looks inside
"It doesn't matter"

It doesn't matter how many fabulous trips I take
Or how much money that I make
"It doesn't matter"

None of these matter if I'm not complete
Peace only begins when God delivers me

Surrender

Take my hand, don't let it go
For I don't want to fear this world no more

Remove all the bad things inside of me
and let that light shine where it needs to be

The troubles of my life have multiplied
but I have faith that you won't let me die

I've stumbled and I've failed when pleasing you
but I know that the storm will blow over
and you will pull me through

I've repented and you've forgiven me so many times
and I've asked for you to restore my mind

My heart is heavy and my body has become weak
I need for you to strengthen me and
make me complete

You said we walk my faith and not by sight
Although things may look crazy right now
I know in my heart that you will
make everything all right

For you said in your word that you will take care of me
"I'm ready Lord, take my hand and
let me walk with Thee"

Walk With Me

Bit by bit, He broke me down to see if I believed
Time after time, He picked me up,
yet I continue to do sinful deeds
Day by day He removed a part of His loving hands
Hour by hour I would get weak and
it was difficult to stand
Minute by minute, I failed to realize that
this was all in His plans
Another day went by, again He removed
another part of His hands
Second by second He kept me breathing
as my life fell into pieces
Because I failed to understand what was
behind all of His reasons
The next day went by, He shook His head as
He began to remove the other hand
He looked at me with tears in His eyes, and asked,
"Child when are you going to understand"

The light bulb came on and finally
I completely understood
I needed to be broken down if I didn't
believe Him like I should
So I stretched out my hands and placed
it in His before it faded away
I said, "Father, I am ready now,
go on and lead the way"

As He took my hand, I could feel my life
being put back together
I knew then that He broke me down just
so I can see Him clearer
While holding His hands, I looked into His
amazing beautiful eyes
My heart skipped a beat because I saw myself
and it caught me my surprise
As He looked down at me, He smiled, and
placed my hand over His heart
He said, "Child all I wanted you to do
was follow me from the start"

Ⳋ

He will teach us his ways, so that we may walk in his paths
Micah 4:2

I stand proud and tall, because
I'm grateful for my falls
Without my stumbles and failures,
I may not have endured them all

I was built to receive all my hurt
and all my pain
I've weathered the storms,
God's strength I retain

I live on the word and feed it into my soul
I don't give the enemy enough
room to take control

I've been attacked by the world and
its surrounding outcomes
But I continue to keep my head up,
because I know God's Will, will be done

I don't need to fight my battles,
mean words I shall not use
I just turn my head towards my Father
and let Him do as He choose

I've learned to appreciate the
words of the gospel
He said that, no weapons that are formed
against me shall prosper

So in the midst of my trials, I stand
still in His peace
Because I know the enemy can't win,
his warfare shall cease

I've accepted the authority God has given me
And I will get what He has in store for me

I will speak power into total full capacity
Because I walk by faith, not by what I see

I will get my inheritance, just as Adam did
Remember I was the creation from his rib

So when I smile, know that it is real
When I hug, know that it is true
When I dance, know that it is for Him,
for delivering me through
I am who I am and I am so proud to be
A woman of God

A Woman Walking Worthy

Beauty...

And provide for those who grieve in Zion
To bestow on them a crown of beauty instead of ashes;
the oil of gladness instead of mourning
a garment of praise instead of a spirit of despair
They will be called oaks of righteousness
A planting of the Lord for the display of his splendor
Isaiah 61:3

Pure Beauty

I'm as beautiful as you think I am
I'm as beautiful as you want me to be

I could have all the beauty on the outside
What matters is the beauty that lies within me

The Beauty of
Love
Joy
And Integrity

True Reflection

When I laugh
Dark days turn sunny

When I smile
Milk turns to sweet honey

When I walk
I walk with pride
Glowing passionately as I stride

When I dress
I dress with class
Wearing the finest clothes and carrying
the best handbags

The length of my hair is the strength of my soul
Turning silver into pure gold

My culture is revealed by the texture of my skin
I can make my worst enemy become my best friend

All these qualities others may see
But true beauty is God's love inside of me

A Black
Woman's Beauty

From the smile on my face
To the fullness of my lips
From the sway of my walk
To the curves of my hips

From the shape of my eyes
To the structure of my cheeks
From the depth of my dimples
That make them so unique

From the natural oil on my body
That makes it so smooth
To the herbs that are engraved
To gravitate moods

From the top of my head
To the bottom of my feet
From the passion that I have
To move you as I speak

From the texture of my hair
To the color of my skin
From the warmth of my heart
That purifies beauty within
I am without a doubt

A Black Woman

A Single Mother's Beauty

I've given you things that money can't buy
I've bathed you and soothed you while
I watched you cry

I've carried your burdens and I've taken your pain
I've covered your body, while mine got wet in the rain

I've starved myself so that you could eat
I've given you my strength while I became weak

I've worked overtime so that you can have
things that are nice
I've given you my last dime and didn't
complain about the price

I made sure that you're well educated
and well behaved
Your mannerism and compassion to you I gave

I took care of you alone there wasn't anybody else
Your father he was long gone, I raised you myself

Yet I'm not complaining because it
was all worth the time
You're growing up very well and
you're doing perfectly fine

Beauty of a Mother's Love

Love shines in you
I've seen its beauty everyday
You have a loving heart
That nobody can take away
You've forgiven so many times
You never turned your back away
You make sure that everyone is fine
And your solution is to always pray
You've gone above and beyond
You do your best to help others out
I can only hope to be as great as you
Because you're the perfect example of
what a mother is about

A Woman's Desire

A woman's desire is to make her family strong
To wake up every morning knowing
that her house is a home
A home where there is laughter, peace, and joy
A place where she can express herself
and others may enjoy

A woman's desire is to raise her children
up in the ways of the Lord
To instill in them the passion for Christ and to know
that the enemy destroys
So that no matter where they go, they would always know
To lean and trust in God always and foremost

A woman's desire is to be a friend and
lover to her spouse
To feel that she's loved all times without
having any doubts
And for him to fulfill his position as being
the head of the house
To be someone who also worships God
with praises and shouts

A woman's desire is to be enriched in the
Lord as her personal Savior
So that no matter how rough life may get,
she remembers to humble her behavior
To always dwell in Him through
good and bad times
And for others to see in her
that it is He who shines

The Core

To believe in our destiny
To know our purpose
To embrace in our passion
To watch our dreams surface
To capture our desire
To sustain in our faith
To live to inspire
To love instead of hate
To receive the award
That proudly awaits

Dig Deep

The roots of a tree where the stem lies
The soar of eagles as they fly
In the peaceful beauty of the clear blue skies

Dig Deep

The blood of passion running through our veins
Under the skin of life, where only tissue remains

Dig Deep

The scars that are marked by a fatal past
The scorn of a woman whose beauty didn't last

Dig Deep

The inevitable transgression of a brutal life
The dignity and identity of a person taken by strife

Dig Deep

The image that is bitter and cannot be consoled
Is overflowed with emotions and it's hard to control

Dig Deep

The evident of a soul that is so pure and innocent
Being deceived by the wicked and deprived of intelligence

Dig Deep

The finish line that is yet so hard to get through
Comes with bumps and curves to hinder you

Dig Deep

The strength of faith that keeps us focus
Is blessed at the end and given a huge token

Dig Deep

Faith...

If you have faith as small as a mustard seed
You can say to the mountain
Move and it will move
Nothing will be impossible for you
Matthew 17:20

Believe the Unseen

Even though I'm someone you cannot see
Do you believe and trust in me
Even though I'm someone you cannot touch
Do you believe that there is such
Even though I'm someone you may not hear
Do you still believe that I am near
When your heart is heavy and filled with sorrow
Do you believe that I will give
you a better tomorrow
Do you depend on me or do you depend on man
Do you believe that man can do what I can
Just in case you have any doubts
This is what I'm all about
See, I made the moon, the sun, and the rain
I gave you pleasure before there was pain
I gave you life before there was death
I created man when I gave him my breath
The house you have and the car you drive
I gave you the health and strength
in order for you to buy
The spouse you have and the children you made
It was all in my plans, to you I gave
That conscious you have when you're
not doing right
It is me whispering in your ear, even though
I may be out of sight
To choose the world instead of me, you've
got it all twisted you see
The world can't give you life for eternity
So loving the world before you love me
Stop think about
WHO'S THE ALMIGHTY

You Better Know

Jesus can move mountains
He can remove pain
Just look to Him
And call out His name

Don't be ashamed, He loves you
Just reach for His hand to hold onto
As long as you stay focused and keep your eyes on Him
There's no chance in hell that the enemy can win

Because of You

Because of you, I was born into this sinful world,
They judged my mother of being an unwed pregnant girl
Because of you, I thirst for forty days and forty nights,
Not a piece of bread or person in sight

Because of you, I healed the sick and fed the poor,
I took care of every need that came knocking at my door
Because of you, they believed and see
That the power of God manifested in me

Because of you, I was falsely accused,
Beaten, spit on, walk in my shoes
Because of you, they put nails through my hands and feet
Would you have done the same for me

Because of you, my father sacrificed me,
So that you may live for eternity
Because of you, I laid on the cross and died for your sins
Would you have done that for me
I don't think so my friend

Because of you, I arose again
To let you know who I was and that all power is in my hands
Because of you, I went through all these
things for you to see,
That the love of God is within me

Now I ask, because of me, would you give your life,
as a living sacrifice, as I have done for you
Or would you turn away from me and walk with strife,
the way Satan wants you to do

Get It Right

The time is now to get it right
He may come during the day
He may come during the night
Seek Him now before it too late
Tear down the walls of pride and hate
He died for you
Do it for His sake

Free...

It is for freedom that Christ has set us free
Stand firm, then, and do not let yourselves
be burdened again by a yoke of slavery
Galatians 5: 1

"We know the works of the devil and how he can be
He is of evil, filled with bondage and captivity
Get to know, Jesus whose love is greater than the enemy
He is the most High, who sets the devil's captives free"

I'm not who you say I am
I'm not where you said I'll be
I'm not here to please you
I'm here to live for me
I'm entertaining the path
That I now see clearly
My eyes are open now

I'm *"Free To Be Me"*

&

I'm as free as the wind blows
I'm as free as the stars in the sky

I'm as free as the water flows
I'm as free as the ocean on high tides

I'm as free as the birds in the air
I'm as free as loose kites

I'm as free as love and care
I'm as free as the passion of Christ

I Am Free....

Peace of Mind
Humbled Soul
Joy of Laughter
All that God Controls

Freedom of Speech
Freedom of Prayer
Freedom of Love
To shine Everywhere

Rebirth...

He saved us, not because of righteous things we had done,
but because of his mercy
He saved us through the washing of rebirth and renewal by the
Holy Spirit, whom he poured out on us generously
through Jesus Christ our Savior, so that,
having been justified by his grace, we might become
heirs having the hope of eternal life
Titus 3:5-7

Listen

Listen to the voice...
That speaks loud and clear
That keeps you from danger and takes away fear

Listen to the voice...
That takes your mind away
From evil thoughts and a bad day

Listen to the voice...
That keeps you sane
That keeps you from crying out in pain

Listen to the voice...
That soothes your soul
That keeps your emotions under control

Listen to the voice...
That sends powerful force
That gives you lessons of each day's course

Listen to the voice...
That loves you
That understands what you're going through

Listen to the voice...
That ignores the flesh
That speaks to you spiritually among all the rest

Let them give thanks to the Lord for his unfailing love
and his wonderful deeds for men,
for he breaks down gates of bronze and cuts through bars of iron
Psalm 107: 13-16

"I'm Coming Out"

Unlock my arms
Unstrap my feet
Move out the way
I have goals to reach

I've renewed my mind
I've freed my soul
It's time that I am in control

There's no more looking back
There's no more sorrow
In fact, I'm looking forward
for tomorrow

There's no more bondage
There's no more pain
I've found myself
My strength I've regain

I'm ready for the world
There's no more fear
I'm free now
I'm not staying here

So step aside
Because I'm stepping out
It's time for the world to know
What I'm all about

I love the Lord, for he heard my voice
He heard my cry for mercy
Because he turned his ear to me,
I will call on him as long as I live
Psalm 116: 1-2

Breinigsville, PA USA
28 September 2009
224872BV00003B/3/P